P9-CKJ-180

ISBN 1 85103 319 X
Originally published as *Jean-Sébastien Bach Découverte des Musiciens* jointly by Editions Gallimard Jeunesse & Erato Disques.

This edition first published in the United Kingdom jointly by Moonlight Publishing Ltd, The King's Manor, East Hendred, Oxon OX12 8JY
& The Associated Board of the Royal Schools of Music (Publishing) Limited, 24 Portland Place, London W1B 1LU.

Printed in Italy

Johann Sebastian

BACH

FIRST DISCOVERY – MUSIC

Written by Paule du Bouchet
Illustrated by Charlotte Voake
Narrated by Michael Cantwell

Johann Sebastian Bach was born into a family of musicians on the first day of Spring 1685. In German, 'Bach' means a stream or little river. His great-great-grandfather, who was a baker, loved to play the cittern, an instrument rather like a guitar.

Bach was born in the little town of Eisenach in the centre of Germany.

LISTEN

Have you ever noticed how tuneful water can be at a mill-wheel or in a stream. Just think how fine it would sound when accompanied by an instrument.

1 BRANDENBURG CONCERTO NO. 5, BWV 1050, 1ST MOVEMENT, ALLEGRO
PRELUDE IN C MAJOR, BWV 939

Johann Sebastian's father is the town musician. He writes music for all the celebrations and festivals in the town. His father's brother Johann Christoph is an organist. His own eldest brother, also called Johann

YOUR TURN TO SING

When the Bach family got together, they loved to sing rounds. Have you ever done this with your friends? One of you begins then the others join in, one after another, from the start of the same tune. All the parts fit together beautifully, and it is great fun singing together.

Christoph, plays the organ too. Many of his other relations are also musical, and the whole Bach family often get together in each other's houses to sing.

Johann Sebastian has a very good voice and sings in his school choir. Every Sunday the Bach family perform music in church. Johann Sebastian's father plays the

LISTEN TO THE ECHO

Have you ever heard music played in a church? Have you noticed how deep and solemn it sounds? Try singing sometime in an empty church, or in any other large stone building with a high ceiling. Listen to how your voice echoes and how long the sounds last.

3 THE SAINT MATTHEW PASSION, BWV 244, CHORALE 'O LORD, WHO DARES TO SMITE THEE?'

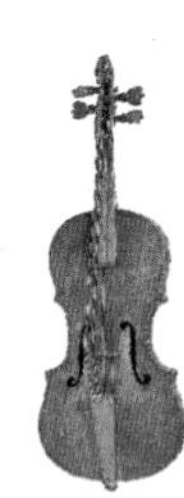

violin, his father's brother is on the organ and little Johann Sebastian sings with his beautiful clear voice. He is already fascinated by the sound of the organ.

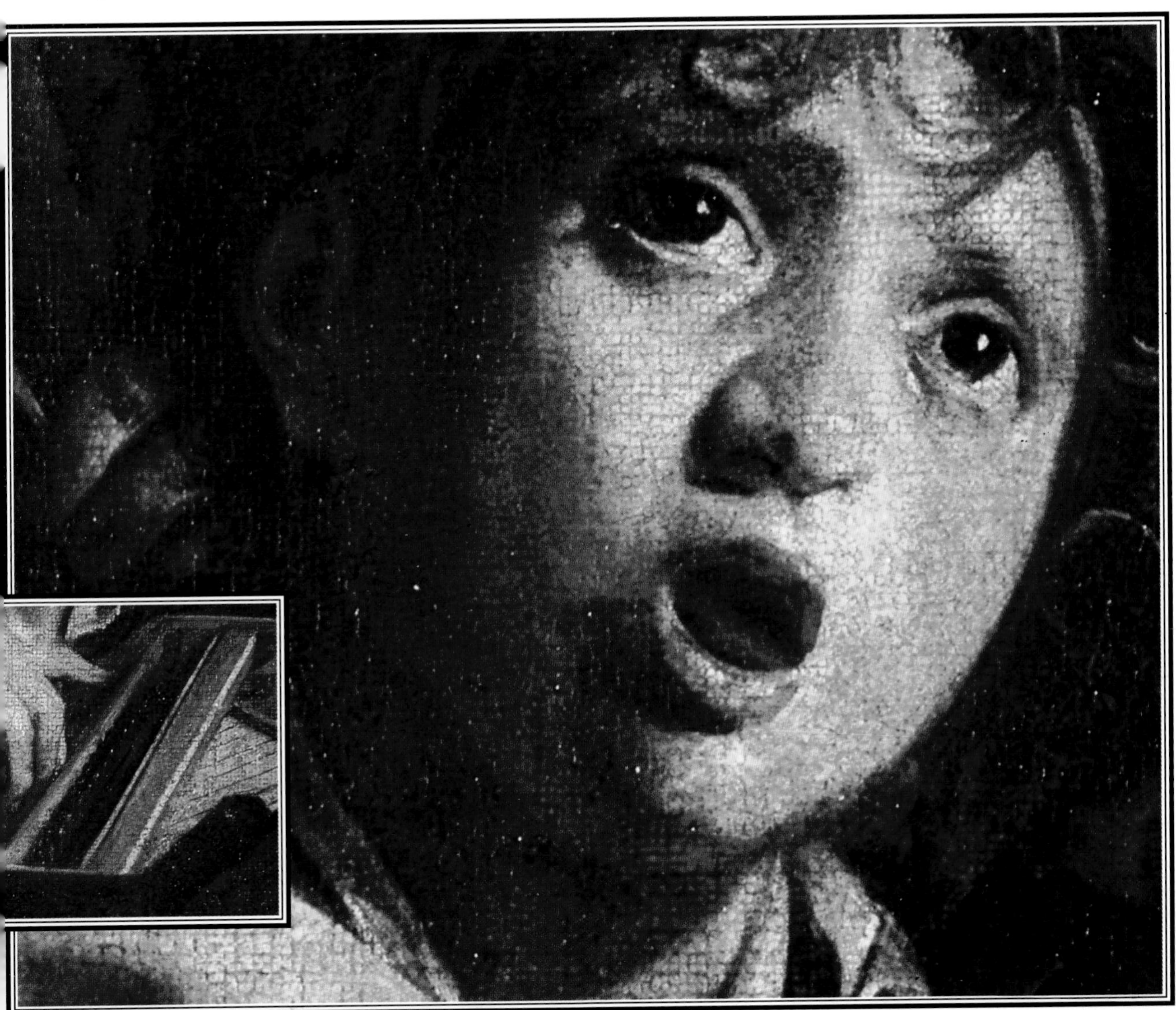

However, when Johann Sebastian is only nine years old, his mother and father both die. He goes to live with his eldest brother Johann Christoph, the organist, and his wife and baby. They are a poor family but Johann

DO YOU LIKE DANCING?

Do you know that one of the best reasons for playing music is so people can dance? Try making up a dance for yourself to suit any music you happen to hear.

Sebastian is a happy child. Although life is hard, there are plenty of happy occasions with singing and dancing in village life at this time.

A SECRET NOTEBOOK

Johann Sebastian loves music. One day he discovers in a cupboard a secret notebook belonging to his brother. In it he finds music written by some of the greatest composers of the time. For nights on end he

5 CANTATA 'SLEEPERS, AWAKE', BWV 140, INTRODUCTION TO THE CHORALE

copies out the music by candlelight. But one night his brother surprises him and angrily takes away the notebook. Johann Sebastian is very unhappy but all the music he has copied is now in his head.

Bach composed a huge amount throughout his life. He wrote his music down by hand with a quill pen.

MUSICAL MEMORY

Can you remember a piece of music you have heard only once? Try to hum or whistle the tune you are about to hear, which is one of the most famous Bach wrote.

At thirteen, Johann Sebastian wants to earn his living. He applies to the best singing school in the country. His voice is so beautiful that he is accepted at once and the teachers give

AT THE VIOLIN MAKER'S

Bach loved the violin and the viola. Have you ever been to a workshop where string instruments are made? If you come across an instrument-maker's shop, ask if you can see some of the instruments made there.

 SONATA FOR VIOLIN AND HARPSICHORD, BWV 1017, LARGO

him a free place at the school. But a year later his voice breaks and he can no longer sing in the choir. Instead he plays his favourite instruments: the organ and the harpsichord, as well as the violin and the viola.

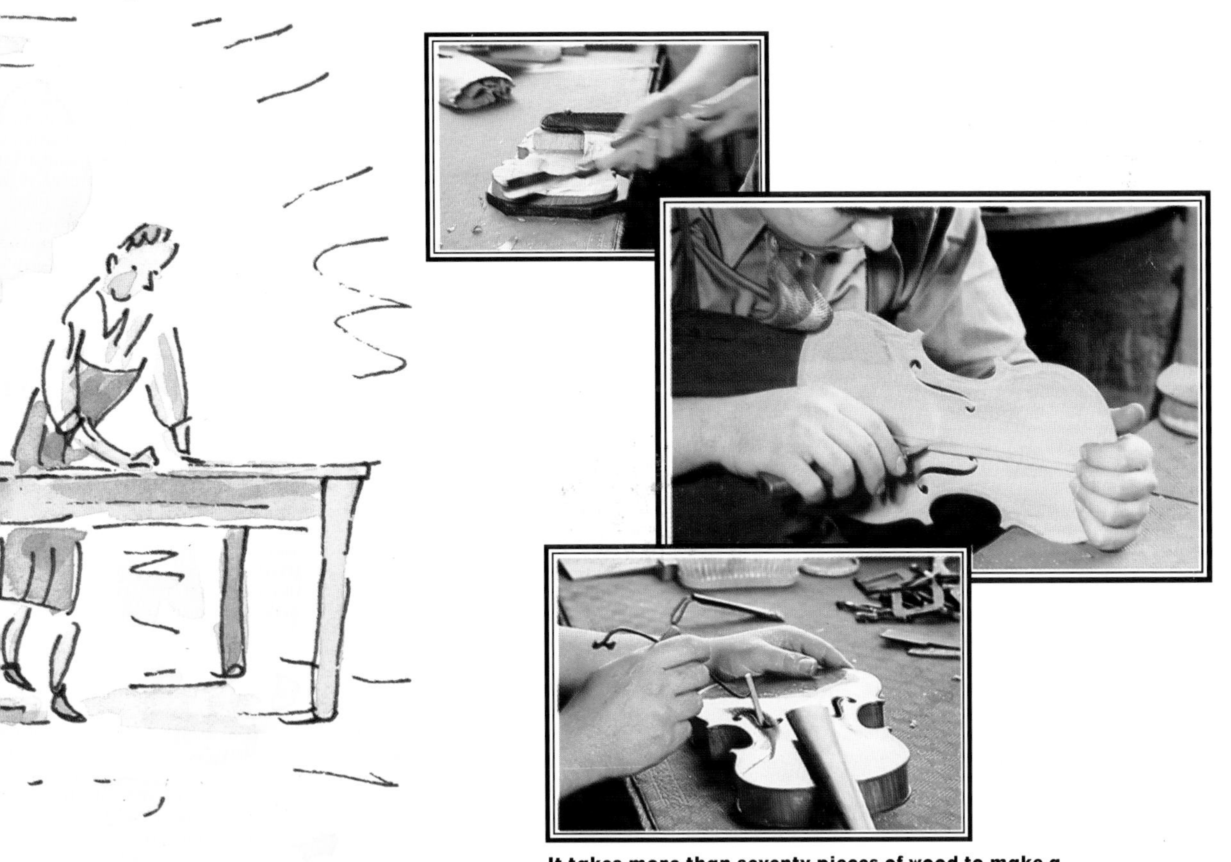

It takes more than seventy pieces of wood to make a violin! Here we see the violin maker hollowing out the sound board (the front) and cutting two f-shaped holes, vital for the quality of sound. In the third photo he is inserting the sound post (a little wooden rod which helps transfer the sound vibrations) in the violin.

One day, when he is eighteen, Johann Sebastian is asked to play on the new organ in the town of Arnstadt. Many people have gathered to listen. Johann Sebastian lets his hands fly over the keys and his feet dance on the pedals. Everyone is

astounded! Never have they heard such sounds. The music seems to come straight from heaven. Johann Sebastian is immediately made organist at Arnstadt. It's his first real job. It is the beginning of his long life playing and composing music.

THE LITTLE STAIRCASE TO THE ORGAN

Have you ever climbed the little staircase which leads to the organ loft in a church? Try it one day when you hear someone playing the organ. From below you can't tell where the music is coming from because you can't see the organist. Go up and visit him or her one day and watch how the organ is played with both hands and feet. The organist will usually be pleased to see you.

Johann Sebastian marries his cousin Maria Barbara and they have seven children. But Maria Barbara dies so young that he then marries Anna Magdalena and lives with her until he dies in 1750. Altogether he has twenty children, ten who live to be grown-up, four of whom become great musicians.

HAVE YOU EVER MADE UP A TUNE?

Bach's children wrote music when they were very young. The piece you are about to hear was made up by Carl Philipp Emanuel when he was ten. His father helped him to write it out. You don't have to know how to write music to make up a tune. You only need to like singing.

Today

as in the past

Bach's

music

is played

and loved.

THE SAINT MATTHEW PASSION

Bach wrote a great deal of sacred music – music for and about God. It was actually part of his job to write music for church services every Sunday: this music included cantatas and passions. Cantatas are like great prayers to the glory of God. Passions recount the story of Jesus Christ's death. Each singer has a role in these choral works. The choir represents the crowds of people, while the soloists play the parts of Jesus, Pontius Pilate, Mary the mother of Jesus or the narrator. The music is always telling a story of some sort. In the cantata you are about to hear, the music portrays the suffering of man on earth and asks God to help him live. The Saint Matthew Passion begins with the arrest of Jesus and ends with his death on the cross. In this magnificent final chorus Jesus has just died and the crowd is weeping.

In his first four years as Cantor at St Thomas's Church, Leipzig (see right), Bach wrote cantatas for every week of the church year.

Bach composed more than 300 cantatas and three magnificent passions.

9 CANTATA, BWV 199, SOPRANO ARIA
THE SAINT MATTHEW PASSION, BWV 244, FINAL CHORUS

THE 'GOLDBERG' VARIATIONS

Bach was a music teacher as well as a composer. He taught the organ and the harpsichord. He taught his own children and had other pupils as well. He was loved by his pupils and he wrote simple music specially for them: the Little Organ Book for his organ pupils and the Little Keyboard Book for his son Wilhelm Friedemann when he was ten. Listen to this minuet written by Bach for his wife Anna Magdalena, who was learning the harpsichord. It is still played by pupils learning the piano. Bach also composed more difficult pieces like The Well-Tempered Clavier or the 'Goldberg' Variations, which he wrote for Johann Goldberg, one of his harpsichord pupils.

After Bach married Anna Magdalena in 1721, he compiled two books of pieces to use in her keyboard lessons. These pieces are still played by pupils learning the piano (right) today.

As Cantor at the church and choir school of St Thomas in Leipzig, Bach was responsible for teaching fifty-five choirboys.

THE LITTLE KEYBOARD BOOK FOR ANNA MAGDALENA BACH: ANON., MINUET IN D MINOR, BWV ANH. II 132; 'GOLDBERG' VARIATIONS, BWV 988, ARIA

THE BRANDENBURG CONCERTOS

Chamber music is music played by a group of musicians in a large room at home like a private concert. Bach wrote nearly all his chamber music when he worked for the Prince of Anhalt-Cöthen, who was a great music lover. He wrote the wonderful Cello Suites and the Violin Partitas, which are amongst the most difficult pieces that cellists and violinists have to play. Listen to this movement from a suite for cello. Doesn't it make you want to play the cello or to dance along with the music? Bach also wrote pieces for bigger groups of instrumentalists, including the Orchestral Suites and the famous Brandenburg Concertos. Just listen to the joy of this concerto.

Bach also wrote marvellous sonatas for pairs of instruments: violin and harpsichord, flute and harpsichord, or viola da gamba and harpsichord.

11 SUITE NO. 5 FOR CELLO, BWV 1011, GIGUE
BRANDENBURG CONCERTO NO. 4, BWV 1049

MOONLIGHT PUBLISHING

Translator:
Penelope Stanley-Baker

ABRSM (PUBLISHING) LTD

Project manager:
Leslie East

Language consultant:
Cathy Ferreira

Text editor:
Lilija Zobens

Editorial supervision:
Caroline Perkins & Rosie Welch

Production:
Simon Mathews & Michelle Lau

English narration recording:
Ken Blair of BMP Recordings

ERATO DISQUES

Artistic and Production Director:
Ysabelle Van Wersh-Cot

LIST OF ILLUSTRATIONS

KEY: **t** = top **m** = middle **b** = bottom
r = right **l** = left

PHOTOGRAPHIC ACKNOWLEDGEMENTS

Agostino Pacciani/Enguerand **22br**. Alban Larousse/Gallimard **6**. Archiv für Kunst und Geschichte, Paris **14tr**, **20**, **21**, **23**, **24**
27. Archives Gallimard Jeunesse **11t**, **14l**, **26t**. Colette Masson/Enguerand **22bl**. D.R. **25**. Édimédia **10–11**. Germanischen Nationalmuseum, Nuremberg **8**. Giraudon **24t**. Jean-Paul Dumontier **18**. Jeunesses musicales de France **17**. Photo Josse **22t**. Ph
Michel Szabo **26b**. Pierre-Marie Valat **24br**.

CD

1. A stream of musicians
Brandenburg Concerto No. 5, BWV 1050, 1st movement, Allegro
The Amsterdam Baroque Orchestra
Director and harpsichord, Ton Koopman
4509 99636 2
℗ Erato Classics SNC, Paris, France 1985 WDR

Prelude in C major, BWV 939
Philippe Castaigns, piano
℗ Erato Disques S.A., Paris, France 1998

2. Music in the family
Motet 'Singet dem Herrn', BWV 225
Monteverdi Choir
English Baroque Soloists
Conducted by John Eliot Gardiner
2292 45979 2
℗ Erato Classics SNC, Paris, France 1982

3. The voice of an angel
The Saint Matthew Passion, BWV 244, Chorale 'Wer hat dich so geschlagen'
Ensemble Vocal de Lausanne
Orchestre de Chambre de Lausanne
Conducted by Michel Corboz
2292 45375 2
℗ Erato Classics SNC, Paris, France 1983

4. Joy and sorrow
Overture to Orchestral Suite No. 1, BWV 1066, Minuet
English Baroque Soloists
Conducted by John Eliot Gardiner
4509 91800 2
℗ Erato Classics SNC, Paris, France 1985

5. A secret notebook
Cantata 'Wachet auf, ruft uns die Stimme', BWV 140, Introduction to the chorale
Scottish Chamber Orchestra
Scottish Philharmonic Singers
Conducted by Raymond Leppard
4509 99634 2
℗ Erato Classics SNC, Paris, France 1984

6. From voice to violin
Sonata for violin and harpsichord, BWV 1017, Largo
Josef Suk, violin
Zuzana Ruzickova, harpsichord
4509 94575 2
℗ Erato Classics SNC, Paris, France 1969

7. Heavenly music
Toccata in D minor, BWV 565
Marie-Claire Alain, organ
4509 99635 2
℗ Erato Classics SNC, Paris, France 1981

8. Some years later
The Little Keyboard Book for Anna Magdalena Bach: C. P. E. Bach, March in D major, H. 1.1
Georges Pludermacher, piano
0630 16244 2
℗ Erato Disques S.A., Paris, France 1996

9. Sacred music
Cantata 'Mein Herz schwimmt in Blut', BWV 199, Aria 'Stumme Seufzer, stille Klagen'
Barbara Schlick, soprano
Marcel Ponseele, oboe
The Amsterdam Baroque Orchestra
Conducted by Ton Koopman
0630 12598 2
℗ Erato Disques S.A., Paris, France 1995

The Saint Matthew Passion, BWV 244, Chorus 'Wir setzen uns mit Tränen nieder'
Ensemble Vocal de Lausanne
Orchestre de Chambre de Lausanne
Conducted by Michel Corboz
2292 45375 2
℗ Erato Classics SNC, Paris, France 1983

10. Bach as teacher
The Little Keyboard Book for Anna Magdalena Bach: Anon., Minuet in D minor, BWV Anh. II 132
Georges Pludermacher, piano
0630 16244 2
℗ Erato Disques S.A., Paris, France 1996

'Goldberg' Variations, BWV 988, Aria
Ton Koopman, harpsichord
0630 14455 2
℗ Erato Classics SNC, Paris, France 1988

11. Chamber music
Suite No. 5 for cello, BWV 1011, Gigue
Jörg Baumann, cello
0630 12333 2
℗ Teldec Classics International GMBH 1984

Brandenburg Concerto No. 4, BWV 1049, 1st movement, Allegro
The Amsterdam Baroque Orchestra
Conducted by Ton Koopman
0630-14453 2
℗ Erato Classics SNC, Paris, France 1985 WDR

FIRST DISCOVERY – MUSIC

JOHANN SEBASTIAN BACH
LUDWIG VAN BEETHOVEN
HECTOR BERLIOZ
FRYDERYK CHOPIN
CLAUDE DEBUSSY
GEORGE FRIDERIC HANDEL
WOLFGANG AMADEUS MOZART
HENRY PURCELL
FRANZ SCHUBERT
ANTONIO VIVALDI